Famous Black Americans

Primary

Save time and energy planning thematic units with this comprehensive resource. We've searched the 1990–1998 issues of **The MAILBOX**® and **Teacher's Helper**® magazines to find the best ideas for you to use when teaching a thematic unit about famous Black Americans. Included in this book are favorite units from the magazines, single ideas to extend a unit, and a variety of reproducible activities. Pick and choose from these activities to develop your own complete unit or simply to enhance your current lesson plans. You're sure to find everything you need right here in this book to create a world of cross-curricular learning experiences for your students.

Editors:
Kimberly Fields
Karen A. Brudnak

Artist:
Teresa R. Davidson

Cover Artist:
Kimberly Richard

www.themailbox.com

©2000 by THE EDUCATION CENTER, INC.
All rights reserved.
ISBN# 1-56234-352-1

Manufactured in the United States
10 9 8 7 6 5 4 3

Table Of Contents

Thematic Units

More Activities And Ideas

Reproducible Activities

Thematic Units...

from **The MAILBOX®** magazine.

CELEBRATING BLACK HISTORY MONTH

This February as you celebrate Black History Month, honor the achievements of black women. The following activities and reproducibles introduce a few of these remarkable women and their contributions to our country.

ideas contributed by Linda D. Rourke

A WINNING POET

Introduce students to Gwendolyn Brooks, winner of the 1950 Pulitzer Prize for poetry. Gwendolyn began writing original poetry at a young age. When she was 15, she sent one of her poems to a poet. The poet responded with words of praise and encouragement. He even gave Gwendolyn a few tips. In 1945, Gwendolyn's first book of poetry, *Bronzeville Boys and Girls,* was published. Her second book of poems, *Annie Allen,* won her the Pulitzer Prize.

Gwendolyn's first book of poetry expresses the feelings of children. One poem is about a boy who envies a tree because the tree will never have to move—something he has had to do seven times. Make a list of events that have recently happened to your students; then list their reactions alongside the events. You'll create a poem that your children are sure to enjoy!

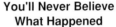

**You'll Never Believe
What Happened**
Lost my sweater—oh no!
Made a new friend—lucky me!
Ate a plate of peas—yuck!
Earned a sticker—hooray!
Talked to my grandpa—funny!

THE PIONEER OF BLACK DANCE

Katherine Dunham—dancer, choreographer, anthropologist—used her many talents to give the world an important gift. Katherine's love for dance evolved early in life. By age 14, she had organized her own dance group. But it was a trip to the West Indies as a student of anthropology that changed Katherine's life. There she was inspired by the beautiful cultural dances. These dances made her realize she could use the language of dance to teach people about black history and culture, and about themselves. Though Katherine no longer performs today, many of the dances she created are still performed.

Compile a list of feelings such as happy, sad, lonely, frightened, courageous; then, in an open area, challenge students to arrange a series of dance movements to express each feeling. Encourage students to make their own music. Then let the show begin! Wouldn't Katherine be proud?

THE QUEEN OF SOUL

Aretha Franklin grew up around beautiful black voices. By the time she had graduated from high school, Aretha knew she wanted to be a professional singer. At age 18, Aretha made a demonstration record for record companies. She also went to a special school to train as a performer. Aretha sang at nightclubs and concerts and made records. But none of the records were best-sellers. It was not until Aretha was allowed to sing "her music" that she became a star. Aretha often accompanies her "soul sound" with her own piano playing.

Aretha once said, "I like life. And I love people. You'll never find me messing with drugs. Life is just too beautiful." Discuss and list the things students feel are beautiful in life. Have each student illustrate one item from the list. Mount the illustrations on a bulletin board entitled "Life Is Beautiful!"

Name _____

A Very Fast Runner

Wilma Rudolph is a real winner! She is a lady who never gives up. Here is her story.

Wilma became very sick when she was a little girl. She had a disease called *polio.* Wilma got better. But she could not walk. So Wilma had to wear a leg brace. Wilma did not like wearing the brace. She wanted to walk on her own. And she really wanted to run. Wilma never gave up. She just kept on trying. Soon Wilma was walking without the brace! Then she was running!

Wilma loved to run. When she had extra time she practiced running. In high school Wilma won many races. Wilma even won an award to go to college. She ran on the college track team. Then, in 1960, Wilma was chosen to run on the Olympic track team! It was there that Wilma proved how great she was. Wilma won three gold medals! No other American woman had ever won three gold medals in track! People called her the world's fastest woman runner.

Read the phrases in each group.
Number the phrases to show the correct order.

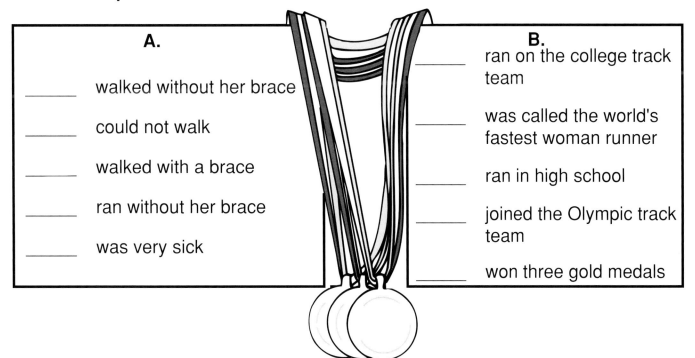

A.

_____ walked without her brace

_____ could not walk

_____ walked with a brace

_____ ran without her brace

_____ was very sick

B.

_____ ran on the college track team

_____ was called the world's fastest woman runner

_____ ran in high school

_____ joined the Olympic track team

_____ won three gold medals

Bonus Box: On the back of this sheet write a sentence telling about something you hope to do one day. Then think about Wilma's story, and write what you think Wilma would tell you to do.

Name _____

What A Lady!

As a little girl, Oprah Winfrey had a dream. She wanted to become an actress. But she never thought her dream could come true. After all, she lived on a pig farm. So how could she become famous?

But Oprah's dream did come true. Today Oprah Winfrey is famous. She is an actress and a model. Oprah has her own talk show, too. And she owns a restaurant. Oprah also bought her own film and TV studio. She is an amazing and talented woman. She likes to do many things. And she isn't afraid to try something new. What do you think Oprah will do next?

Find a word from the story for each description below. Write the words on the lines.

1. scared _____

2. an animal _____

3. opposite of few _____

4. a wish _____

5. a lady who acts _____

6. a place to eat _____

7. very well-known _____

8. a person who poses _____

9. small _____

10. rhymes with harm _____

Bonus Box: Oprah likes to do many things. On the back of this sheet list three things you like to do.

Making A Difference

African-American Trailblazers

African-Americans who have dared to fight racism and fulfill their dreams are at the heart of black history. Use these teaching suggestions and the reproducible cards to enrich your celebration of Black History Month.

Calendar Companions

Introduce your students to a variety of famous African-Americans with this pictorial plan. After your daily calendar activity, present a picture of a famous African-American. (To use the 12 portraits on pages 9–12, make a two-sided photocopy of the portrait cards, with the person's picture on one side and the facts about him or her on the other.) As a class discuss the featured African-American and how he or she has influenced the growth and development of our nation. Then showcase the picture near your calendar display. On each day that follows, challenge students to recall the contributions of the famous person(s) on display before introducing that day's featured African-American. By the end of the month, your students will know a wealth of information about famous African-Americans—and you'll also have a striking display!

Amy Hall—After-School Program, Tree House Day Care, Robinson, IL

Something To Talk About

Here's a teaching format that youngsters are sure to love. Pair students and have each twosome research a different African-American. Then ask each pair to present its information in the format of an interview. To do this, one student role-plays an interviewer and the other role-plays the African-American who has been researched. Encourage the students to dress for their parts. These high-interest presentations are sure to bring rave reviews. If possible, videotape the event. Move over Oprah! You've got plenty of competition headed your way!

Pamela Whitted, University School, Johnson City, TN

Charting African-American Contributions

Compile your youngsters' research efforts on an easy-to-read chart like the one shown. As each youngster makes a discovery, write it on the chart. Before long you'll have an abundance of information that can be used in a variety of ways. For example, each student can create a booklet of African-American contributions. To do this a student describes and illustrates a different contribution on each page of a blank booklet. Or challenge students to illustrate things that all people today can do that result from the efforts of African-Americans. Showcase these illustrations and a border of colorful hand cutouts on a bulletin board entitled "Applauding The Contributions Of African-Americans."

Agnes Tirrito—Gr. 2
Kennedy Elementary School
Texarkana, TX

African-American Trailblazers	
Name	Contribution
Rosa Parks	• Civil Rights Activist
Neal Loving	• Aviator
Harriet Tubman	• A Leader of the Underground Railway
Colin Powell	• Chairman of Joint Chiefs of Staff

A Celebration Of Differences

Celebrate the differences among people with this baking project. With your students' help, prepare a batch of your favorite rolled cookie dough. Then, using a cookie cutter, have each child cut out a body shape from the rolled dough. As the cookies bake, talk about how the cookies were made. Guide students to conclude that while the shapes of the cookies may vary, the cookies are all the same on the inside. When the cookies have cooled, ask each student to decorate a cookie to his liking. To encourage creativity, provide several colors of frosting and a wide variety of edible cookie decorations. Have each student display his work of art on a napkin at his desk. Provide time for students to admire their classmates' cookies. Lead the students to conclude that the differences among the cookies make them unique and special. Then, as the youngsters consume their creations, help them apply this important concept to the world around them.

Patsy Blakley—Gr. 2, Haskell Elementary School, Haskell, TX

A Literature Link

Plan to read aloud several inspirational picture books that feature contemporary African-American characters. Here are a few titles that your youngsters are sure to enjoy.

Boundless Grace • *Written by Mary Hoffman & Illustrated by Caroline Binch • Dial Books For Young Readers, 1995*

The spunky heroine of *Amazing Grace* is back! Grace is reunited with her father—a man who left home when Grace was very small and who now lives in Africa. Grace discovers that even though she and her father live on different continents, the two are connected at the heart.

Joshua's Masai Mask • *Written by Dakari Hru & Illustrated by Anna Rich • Lee & Low Books Inc., 1993*

In this modern African-American fable, a young boy realizes that he's proud of his talents and happy to be himself.

Tanya's Reunion • *Written by Valerie Flournoy & Illustrated by Jerry Pinkney • Dial Books For Young Readers, 1995*

This is a heartwarming tale about the beloved characters from *The Patchwork Quilt.* When Tanya and her grandma go to help with preparations for a big family reunion, Tanya learns about the history of the farm where Grandma grew up.

Uncle Jed's Barbershop • *Written by Margaree King Mitchell & Illustrated by James Ransome • Simon & Schuster Books For Young Readers, 1993*

Uncle Jed was a man with a dream. Sarah Jean—his niece and now a grown lady—tells the poignant story of her Uncle Jed, his dream, and what he taught her.

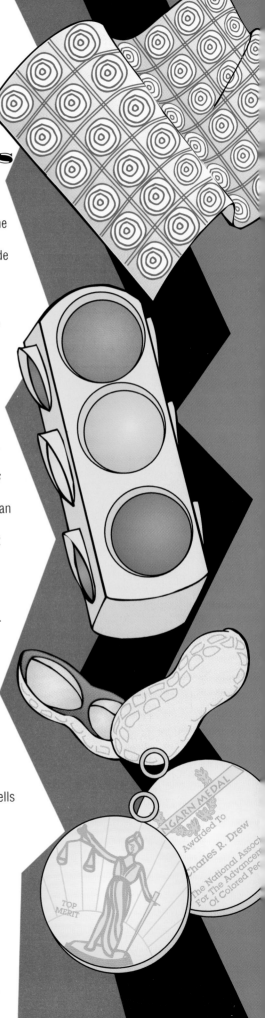

Thurgood Marshall
(1908–1993)

In 1967 Thurgood Marshall became the first Black American to serve on the Supreme Court.

Interesting Fact: In grade school Thurgood was often sent to the principal's office for misbehaving. His punishment was the same each time—staying after school to memorize a different part of the Constitution of the United States. Later in life, Thurgood's knowledge of the Constitution helped him decide on a career in law.

Jackie Joyner-Kersee
(1962–   )

Jackie has won several Olympic gold medals. She is one of the top athletes in the world. Her specialty is track and field.

Interesting Fact: When Jackie was born, her grandmother believed that one day this little baby would be "the first lady of something." So Jackie was named after the nation's first lady at the time—Jacqueline Kennedy.

Marian Anderson
(1897–1993)

In 1955 Marian became the first Black American to sing with the Metropolitan Opera. All her life she used her beautiful singing voice to achieve goals that seemed out of reach for Black Americans.

Interesting Fact: Marian showed great determination even as a child. Without any lessons, Marian taught herself how to play the piano well enough to accompany her own singing!

Bill Cosby
(1937–   )

Bill Cosby is one of America's most cherished comedians and actors. In 1965 he became the first black actor to star in a weekly TV series.

Interesting Fact: Education is a top priority to Bill Cosby. But when he was a teenager, he quit school when he found out that he would have to repeat tenth grade. A few years later he realized his mistake, so he earned his high school equivalency certificate and went to college. Today he is the proud holder of a doctorate in education.

Arthur Ashe, Jr.
(1943–1993)

In 1975, Arthur Ashe became the first Black American to win the prestigious Wimbledon tennis tournament. In addition to playing superb tennis, Arthur continually displayed outstanding sportsmanship.

Interesting Fact: Arthur did much more than win tennis tournaments. He helped children learn to play tennis by establishing inner-city clinics. He also authored several books, spoke out about prejudice, and started a foundation to fight AIDS.

Maya Angelou
(1928–   )

Maya was chosen by President Clinton to write and recite a poem for his presidential inauguration. Her poem was about bringing people of all races together. She is one of America's most famous writers.

Interesting Fact: The name *Maya* is a childhood nickname. It was her brother's way of saying "my sister." Maya—whose real name is Marguerite—has used her special nickname all her life.

Ed Bradley
(1941–   )

Ed Bradley is an American journalist whose work has earned him nearly every significant broadcasting award. He is a coeditor and correspondent of the television news program titled "60 Minutes."

Interesting Fact: After graduating from college, Ed Bradley's first job was teaching sixth grade. He also worked evenings at a radio station for $1.25 per hour. Ed says that his mother—who always told him that he could be anything that he wanted to be—was the biggest influence in his life.

Mae C. Jemison
(1956–   )

When the spacecraft *Endeavour* was launched on September 12, 1992, Dr. Mae C. Jemison became the first Black American woman to explore space.

Interesting Fact: As a child Mae dreamed of becoming an astronaut. But when she went to college, she studied to be a doctor. After medical school she used her skills to help needy people in other countries. When she returned to the United States, Mae still dreamed of becoming an astronaut, and she made that her goal!

Rosa Parks
(1913–   )

Rosa is one of the founders of the civil rights movement. She has spent her lifetime helping to establish equality among people of all races.

Interesting Fact: When Rosa Parks refused to give up her seat on a public bus, she was arrested. Today, in honor of her many accomplishments, an avenue on that same bus route is called "Rosa Parks Boulevard."

George Washington Carver
(1864–1943)

Dr. Carver was a famous scientist who discovered 125 products that could be made using sweet potatoes and more than 300 products that could be made using peanuts.

Interesting Fact: When George graduated from college in 1894, he received a bouquet of flowers from friends. On that day he wore one of the flowers in his buttonhole. It has been written that from that day forward, he always wore a fresh flower.

Neal V. Loving
(1916–   )

Neal Loving was the first Black American and the first double amputee to qualify as a racing pilot.

Interesting Fact: Neal Loving was born in the same city and on the same day of the year as Charles A. Lindbergh, the first pilot to fly solo across the Atlantic Ocean. Both men were born in Detroit, Michigan, on February 4.

Oprah Winfrey
(1954–   )

Oprah Winfrey—talk-show host, actress, producer, humanitarian—is one of today's most successful Black Americans. In 1988 she became the first Black American to own a major TV-and-film-production studio.

Interesting Fact: Just as Oprah has shared her life to help others, she has also shared her wealth. She has given millions of dollars and much of her time to good causes. Oprah hopes to make a difference in her lifetime and to be the best that she can be.

Against All Odds

At the heart of Black History Month are the African-Americans who have dared to fulfill their dreams despite the challenges and obstacles they have faced. Use this beginning research project to introduce your students to a variety of African-American achievers.

Angela Neal, Kingwood, TX

Researching African-American Achievers

Gather an assortment of books featuring biographical information about African-American achievers and display the collection in your classroom. After a few days, display a length of bulletin-board paper titled "African-American Achievers." Ask your students to name men, women, and children who they feel should be listed. Write their ideas and a few of your own on the paper. Then as you distribute copies of the form on page 14, tell students that you would like each of them to research a famous African-American. Encourage students to refer to the class list of African-American Achievers for ideas. Then discuss the research form. Make sure the students understand that they must list on their forms the names of the books and magazines where they find their information. Assign a due date for this portion of the project.

Writing Summary Paragraphs

The next step in the research project will be for students to incorporate the information they have gathered into summary paragraphs. To demonstrate this step, show students a research form that you have completed about a fictitious person; then use the information on the form to create an informative paragraph. Leave the paragraph on display so that students can use it as a model.

An Impressive Display

Display your youngsters' research efforts on a large hallway bulletin board titled "African-American Achievers." Ask each student to illustrate a portrait of his chosen subject on a 9" x 12" sheet of construction paper. To make a poster for the hallway display, each student uses letter stencils to write his subject's name near the top of a length of bulletin-board paper. Then he attaches the portrait he drew and the summary he wrote, adds any other desired decorations, and signs his name. You can count on this impressive display generating a wealth of interest!

Biographies For The Primary Classroom

An increasing number of easy-to-read biographies are being published each year. Peruse this collection of recommended titles, and then enlist the help of your school media specialist in locating the best books for use in your classroom.

Little Louis And The Jazz Band: The Story Of Louis "Satchmo" Armstrong
Written by Angela Shelf Medearis & Illustrated by Anna Rich
Lodestar Books, 1994

Louis "Satchmo" Armstrong taught the world to swing! This is the life story of the man who introduced jazz music to thousands of people. Lively text and expressive illustrations deliver this delightful story about a legendary great. (Another informative title featured in the Rainbow Biography Series is *Dare To Dream: Coretta Scott King And The Civil Rights Movement.*)

A Picture Book Of Harriet Tubman
Written by David A. Adler & Illustrated by Samuel Byrd
Holiday House, Inc.; 1992

This poignant and beautifully illustrated biography is about the remarkable African-American woman who escaped from slavery and became famous as a conductor on the Underground Railroad. Other titles in this biography series include *A Picture Book Of Martin Luther King, Jr.; A Picture Book Of Jesse Owens; A Picture Book Of Frederick Douglass;* and *A Picture Book Of Rosa Parks.*

First Biographies Series: *Booker T. Washington*
Written by Jan Gleiter and Kathleen Thompson & Illustrated by Rick Whipple
Raintree Steck-Vaughn Publishers, 1995

Easy-to-read text accompanied by large and inviting illustrations trace the life of Booker T. Washington from childhood to adulthood.

Biography For Beginners: Sketches For Early Readers
Favorable Impressions; Omnigraphics, Inc.

Written especially for young readers, this unique series offers biographical sketches on people of current interest to children including actors, astronauts, athletes, authors, cartoonists, directors and producers, musicians, political and world leaders, scientists, and television personalities. Each biographical sketch features a current photograph, a quote, and from five to seven pages of easy-to-read information.

AFRO-BETS® Book Of Black Heroes From A To Z
Written by Wade Hudson and Valerie Wilson Wesley
Just Us Books, Inc.; 1988

Forty-nine extraordinary heroes are featured in this easy-to-read children's resource. From Ira Aldridge and Aretha Franklin to Malcolm X and Shaka Zulu, each letter of the alphabet is represented by one or more heroes of African descent. A brief biography, accompanied by a photo or an illustration, profiles each of these historic and contemporary figures.

A Famous Black American

Sojourner Truth

Full name: _____

Date of birth: _____

Place of birth: _____

If this person is no longer living, when did he or she die?

_____

Why is this person famous? _____

_____

_____

Elijah McCoy

List five interesting facts about this person:

1. _____

   _____

2. _____

   _____

3. _____

   _____

4. _____

   _____

5. _____

   _____

Rosa Parks

This information was taken from _____

_____

_____

_____

Thurgood Marshall

A Man With A Dream

On the third Monday in January, America pauses to pay tribute to Dr. Martin Luther King, Jr., and the contributions he made toward achieving peace and racial harmony. Capture student interest in this honorable man with the following activities.

I have a dream that everyone will laugh each day.

Share the following excerpt from one of Dr. King's famous speeches:
"I have a dream that my four little children will one day live in a nation where they will not be judged by the color of their skin but by the content of their character."
Guide students to recognize the importance of Dr. King's dream; then enlist students to create dreams of their own—dreams that could one day provide our world with peace and harmony. Have students complete the sentence starter "I have a dream that...." Students mount their work on large sheets of white construction paper, illustrate their dreams, and trim their completed projects to form cloud shapes. Punch holes and suspend from lengths of colorful yarn or ribbon.

A very peaceful man, Dr. King taught others that changes could be made without the use of violence. Have students propose changes they would like to have happen at home or at school. As a class, determine how these changes could be made without the use of violence. Evaluate each solution and identify the techniques, such as discussion, listening, and understanding, that would be necessary to solve the problem. Point out that these are techniques utilizing the mind and heart rather than the strength of one's body. Conclude the activity by providing each student with a 3-inch construction paper square. Instruct each student to design a "Patch Of Nonviolence" to signal others that he is a peaceful person. When complete, punch a hole in each student's patch; then safety pin it to his clothing.

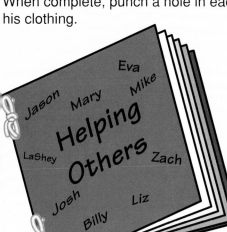

Even when Martin was a boy he knew that he wanted to help others. At a young age Martin made up his mind to become a minister like his father before him. Brainstorm a class list of service careers such as teachers, policemen, firemen, and doctors. Have each student illustrate and label one career from the list. Compile the illustrations into a class book entitled "Helping Others." For a finishing touch, have each student sign his name on the book cover.

Keep Dr. Martin Luther King, Jr.'s dream of freedom alive! Using the following hands-on activities and ready-to-use card center, help students celebrate Dr. King's birthday by practicing his peaceful principles.

Joining Hands For Peace

Dr. King encouraged people to work for what was right in a peaceful way. For his work, he was awarded the Nobel Peace Prize in 1964. Bring the spirit of Dr. King's teachings into your classroom with this inspirational display. Mount a dove cutout and the title "Joining Hands For Peace." Have each student trace his hand and cut out the resulting shape. On his cutout, have each child write his name and how he can help make the classroom a friendly place. Display students' completed projects around the dove cutout. Then attach a yarn length adorned with construction-paper laurel leaves among the cutouts. The display makes a lovely reminder of Dr. King's dream.

Keeping The Dream Alive

Commemorate Dr. King's birthday with the activity cards on pages 17–18. Photocopy and mount the Dr. King artwork on page 19 onto poster board. Then photocopy and cut out the activity cards. Laminate. Attach a 5" x 7" press-on pocket to the back of the Dr. King artwork. Store the activity cards in the pocket.

If desired, have each student complete his activities in a special Dr. King booklet. For each student, duplicate eight copies of the booklet page and one copy of the student management chart (page 21). To make a cover for his booklet, have each student glue his copy of the management chart atop a folded, 9" x 12" sheet of construction paper, then color Dr. King. Assist each student in stapling his booklet pages to his booklet cover. A student completes each activity on a booklet page, then colors the matching star on his booklet cover. The dream *is* still alive!

One And The Same

Dr. King believed *all* people, in spite of their differences, were basically the same and should be treated equally. Make students aware of their basic similarities with this special class booklet. Using the pattern on page 20, duplicate pages for the booklet on white construction paper. To create the first page, cut out and program one copy *We are all alike because....* After a discussion about ways in which all people are similar, distribute a copy of the pattern to each student. Have each student cut out his copy, then write his name and a completion for the sentence. Have him decorate the outline to resemble himself using construction paper and fabric scraps, yarn lengths, crayons, and/or markers.

To assemble, tape the pages together to create an accordion-folded booklet. To showcase your booklet, unfold and display it along a chalk ledge or windowsill.

Cause For Celebration

Celebrate Dr. King's birthday with a special party. Have students use tubes of decorator's icing to decorate a birthday cake for Dr. King; then add a plastic, wedding-cake dove if desired. As students sample their creation, share one of these literature tie-ins:
- *A Picture Book of Martin Luther King, Jr.* by David A. Adler
- *Martin Luther King Day* by Linda Lowery

To conclude the celebration, recognize each student's participation with a copy of the award on page 21. What an inspirational celebration!

Critical thinking activities

Making Dreams Come True

Write your dream for the future.
List three things you can do to make
your dream come true.

Critical thinking activities

A Special Gift

Draw and color a picture of a birthday gift you think
Dr. King would have liked.

Critical thinking activities

Making Changes

Draw and color a picture of something you would like
to change.
Write how you would make this change happen.

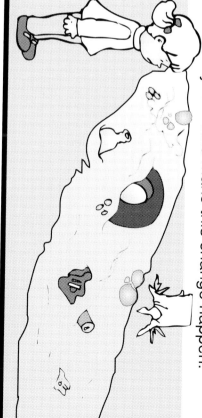

Critical thinking activities

A Happy Event

Patriotism, kindness, and brotherhood made Dr. King
happy.
Write about something that has happened in your
community that would have made Dr. King happy.

All Alike

Draw and color a picture of someone who looks different from you.

Write three ways you and this person are **alike**.

A Peaceful Plan

List three things kids can do to make a community more peaceful.

Working Together

Write about a time you and a classmate worked together.

Have your classmate illustrate it for you.

Solving Problems

Write a problem-solving plan.

Tell how to settle differences on the playground without fighting.

18

Keeping The Dream Alive

Pattern
Use with "One And The Same" on page 16.

Name _____   Booklet page

Student Management Chart

Keeping The Dream Alive

Name _____

1. Making Dreams Come True

2. All Alike

3. Making Changes

4. A Peaceful Plan

5. A Special Gift

6. Working Together

7. A Happy Event

8. Solving Problems

is keeping

Dr. King's dream alive!

Freedom Bell

Martin Luther King, Jr., proclaimed that freedom should ring throughout the country. These colorful bells are a wonderful reminder of Dr. King's wishes. To make a freedom bell, put dollops of red and white tempera paint on a disposable plate. Partially inflate a small balloon to a size that allows it to be held in one hand. Gently press the balloon into the paint; then press the painted balloon surface onto a 9" x 12" sheet of blue construction paper. For a feathery effect, slightly roll the balloon. Paint the surface of the blue paper using the manner described. When the painted paper has dried, trace a bell-shaped template onto the paper and cut along the resulting outline. Hole-punch the top and the bottom of the painted bell shape. On the blank side of the cutout, write a sentence that describes freedom. Thread a jingle bell onto a length of yarn and tie the yarn ends; then attach the jingle bell through the bottom hole in the project. Through the top hole, thread lengths of red, white, and blue curling ribbon. Tie the ribbon lengths and curl the resulting ribbon ends for a festive look. Display clusters of these freedom bells where air currents will occasionally cause them to move. Let freedom ring!

painting technique by Lona Claire Uzueta—Grs. K–1
Play N Learn
Fairbanks, AK

Freedom is making choices!

My Dream
I dream that the children in Bosnia will have peace. I dream that the children in Haiti will have clean water.
by Sarah

Dr. King Mobile

Keep Dr. Martin Luther King's dream alive with these patriotic mobiles. To make a mobile, glue a 5 1/2-inch, red construction-paper circle in the center of a 9-inch white paper plate. Color and cut out a copy of the Dr. King pattern on page 24; then glue the cutout in the center of the red circle. Use a blue marker or crayon to outline the rim of the plate as shown and to draw a large cloud shape on a 9" x 12" sheet of white construction paper. Cut out the cloud shape; then write a dream(s) for our world inside the shape. Hole-punch two holes in the top and bottom of the paper-plate project and in the top of the cloud shape. Thread a 12-inch length of red yarn through the holes at the top of the plate and tie the yarn ends. To connect the cloud cutout to the paper plate, thread a 12-inch length of red yarn through the remaining holes; then tie the yarn ends.

Barbara S. Johnson—Gr. 1, Greensboro Primary School, Greensboro, GA

Black History

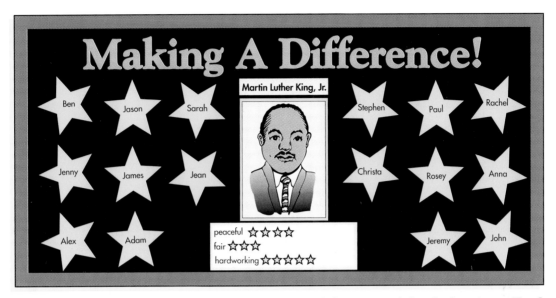

Use this year-round display to promote altruism and foster positive behaviors. Each month showcase a poster or cutout of a person who has contributed to the betterment of others. Add the person's name and a sign that lists his or her most outstanding traits. Then have every student create a personalized cutout for the display. Each time you observe a student or the class exhibiting one of the listed traits, attach a foil star beside that trait. Wow! Look who's making a difference now!

Hope Bertrand—Grs. 2–3, Fremont Elementary School, Bakersfield, CA

As students create this display, they learn about famous Black Americans. Each student researches a different African-American hero or heroine, and writes several interesting facts about him or her. The student mounts his written work atop a slightly larger piece of construction paper. Then he mounts a picture of the famous person he researched on a heart cutout. (The picture may be cut from a discarded periodical, traced and colored by the student, or student-illustrated.) Display the completed projects as shown. Now that's impressive!

Karen Bryant—Gr. 3, Rosa Taylor Elementary School, Macon, GA

As students complete this display, they are reminded of Dr. Martin Luther King, Jr.'s dream for a peaceful world. Using the pattern below, enlarge, color, cut out, and mount a large portrait as shown. Have each student write his name and how he plans to be a peaceful person on a pink paper heart. Display the peaceful thoughts for all to read.

Patterns Use with "Dr. King Mobile" on page 22 and "Keeping His Dream Alive" above.

24

Reproducible Activities...

from Teacher's Helper® magazine.

Background For The Teacher
Black Inventors

Have you ever used an ice-cream scoop? Did you know that it was invented by a black inventor, Alfred Cralle? Many other everyday items that make our lives easier came from the creative minds of ingenious black Americans. These items include:

the lawn sprinkler—J.H. Smith
the fire escape ladder—Joseph Winters
the dustpan—Lloyd Ray
the eggbeater—Willis Johnson
the bicycle frame—Isaac Johnson
the golf tee—George Grant
the player piano—Joseph Dickinson
the horseshoe—Oscar Brown
the refrigerator—John Stanard

For black Americans like Garrett Morgan, who invented the automatic traffic signal, inventions were not isolated events but part of a lifelong devotion to creative problem solving. Mr. Morgan also produced an invention for sewing machines. In 1914 his invention of a practical gas mask earned him a gold medal at the International Exposition Of Sanitation And Safety. In 1916 he used his mask to rescue workmen trapped in a tunnel under Lake Erie. For his bravery he was awarded a gold medal by the city of Cleveland.

Black inventors have generously added to the well-being of many people, and our quality of life has been significantly improved through their efforts.

Note To The Teacher

Use this unit to focus attention on the contributions of black scientists and inventors during Black History Month. Help students to appreciate the unselfish attitude of men and women who invented items to help improve life in general for all people. Black students in particular can develop positive attitudes toward science, knowing that black scientists, as well as black athletes and musicians, have provided ample role models. All students can come to realize that anybody who can think of a better way to do something can be an inventor, even a child!

Materials Needed For Each Child To Make An Inventions Booklet:

one brad
a sharp knife (for teacher's use only) to make slits
a stapler
scissors, glue, crayons, a pencil

How To Use Page 27 (Booklet Pages 1 and 2)

1. Reproduce one copy for each child.
2. Discuss the meaning of the word inventor (a person who makes something based on his imagination). Explain that anyone can be an inventor, including children!
3. Cut the sheet in half on the heavy dotted line.

Booklet Page 1 (lawn sprinkler)

1. Read the text on the first page of the booklet. Note the inventor's name and discuss the use of the lawn sprinkler.
2. Color the page but do not cover the manuscript line. Make blue drops of water all over the page. Cut out and assemble the sprinkler head using a brad pushed through the Xs.
3. Read the sentence starter at the bottom of the page and discuss possible ways of finishing it. Allow the children to write their own endings.

Booklet Page 2 (elevator)

1. Read the text on the second page of the booklet. Note the inventor's name and discuss the uses of the elevator and how it makes our life easier.
2. Color the page but do not cover the manuscript line. Slit the page (with the sharp knife) on the dotted lines indicated with the word cut. Cut out the strip on the side of the page and insert it through the slits so the elevator appears to go up and down when the strip is pulled.
3. Read the sentence starter at the bottom of the page and discuss possible ways of finishing it. Allow the children to write their own endings.

J.H. Smith invented the lawn sprinkler.
Thank you, Mr. Smith!

1

Color and cut.
Assemble with a brad.
Write.

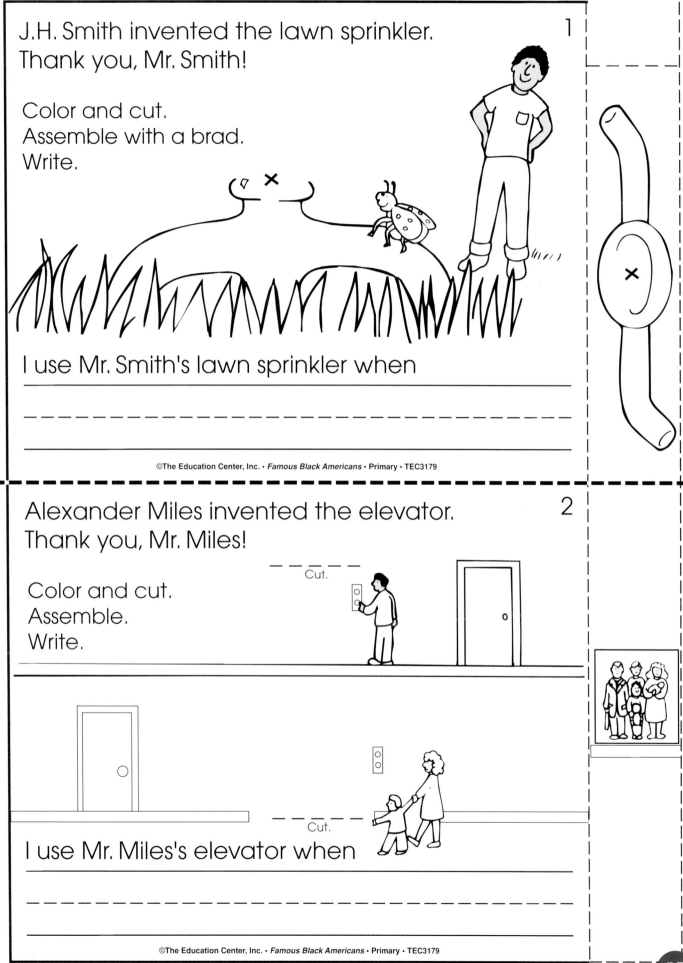

I use Mr. Smith's lawn sprinkler when

_____

_____

_____

Alexander Miles invented the elevator.
Thank you, Mr. Miles!

2

Color and cut.
Assemble.
Write.

Cut.

Cut.

I use Mr. Miles's elevator when

_____

_____

_____

27

How To Use Page 29 (Booklet Pages 3 and 4)

1. Reproduce one copy for each child.
2. Cut the sheet in half on the heavy dotted line.

Booklet Page 3 (refrigerator)

1. Read the text on the third page of the booklet. Note the inventor's name and discuss the uses of the refrigerator, how it makes our life easier, and why it is important to our health.
2. Color the page but do not cover the manuscript line. Cut out the boxes on the right of the page. Let the students decide which items might be found in a refrigerator. Paste them in the refrigerator on the page. Items not found in a refrigerator can be pasted beside the man.
3. Read the sentence starter at the bottom of the page and discuss possible ways of finishing it. Allow the children to write their own endings.

Booklet Page 4 (dustpan)

1. Read the text on the fourth page of the booklet. Note the inventor's name and discuss the use of the dustpan and how it makes our life easier.
2. Complete the dot-to-dot. Color the page but do not cover the manuscript line. Cut out the brush in the box on the right of the page. Paste it near the dustpan. Crumple up some scraps of paper and paste them on the dustpan.
3. Read the sentence starter at the bottom of the page and discuss possible ways of finishing it. Allow the children to write their own endings.

Booklet Cover

1. Reproduce the booklet cover below. Discuss the two additional inventors shown and the importance of their inventions.
2. Allow the children to color and cut out the cover. Cut and paste the traffic light and ironing board in the appropriate thought bubbles.
3. Stack the booklet pages in order and staple the cover on top.

Booklet Cover

Inventions by Black Americans

Garrett Morgan invented the traffic light.

Sarah Boone invented the ironing board.

John Stanard invented the refrigerator.
Thank you, Mr. Stanard!

3

Color.
Cut and paste.
Write.

I use Mr. Stanard's refrigerator

_____

- - - - - - - - - - - - - - - - -

_____

Lloyd Ray invented the dustpan.
Thank you, Mr. Ray!

4

Connect the dots.
Color and cut.
Paste.
Write.

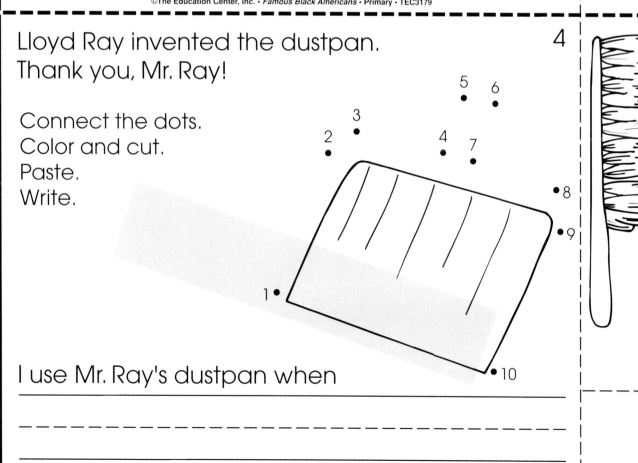

I use Mr. Ray's dustpan when

_____

- - - - - - - - - - - - - - - - -

_____

·········A Parade Of·········
Prominent Black Americans

Background For The Teacher
Martin Luther King, Jr.

Dr. Martin Luther King, Jr., was born in Atlanta, Georgia, on January 15, 1929. King was the son of a Baptist preacher, and he was later ordained a Baptist minister. In 1953, he married Coretta Scott. Together they had four children.

On December 1, 1955, an African-American woman named Rosa Parks refused to give up her bus seat to a white passenger in Montgomery, Alabama. As a result, she was arrested. African-American activists formed an association to boycott the Montgomery transit system. King was chosen by the activists to lead the protest.

Although King's house was bombed and the welfare of his family was threatened, he continued to fight peacefully against segregation. A little over a year later, the boycott ended and the Montgomery transit system was desegregated. King was recognized as a strong leader who worked in nonviolent ways and dreamed of equality for all people.

King continued to lecture all over the country, discussing the plight of African-Americans. Along with his followers, he led marches and demonstrations. On August 28, 1963, a massive civil rights demonstration was held in front of the Lincoln Memorial. Here crowds were uplifted as they listened to King speak of his dream of freedom and equality for all people.

In 1964 the Civil Rights Act authorized the federal government to enforce desegregation of employment and publicly owned facilities. That year closed with King being awarded the Nobel Peace Prize.

On April 4, 1968, King was assassinated in Memphis, Tennessee. The third Monday in January has been declared a federal holiday by the United States Congress so that we may honor King.

How To Use Page 31

To introduce your students to Dr. Martin Luther King, Jr., read aloud the information in "Background For The Teacher" on this page. Then distribute copies of page 31. Direct students to read the story and fill in the missing words.

Happy Birthday, Dr. King

Read the story.
Fill in the missing words.

January 15
☆ ☆ ☆ ☆ ☆ ☆ ☆

King
☆ ☆ ☆ ☆ ☆ ☆ ☆

same
☆ ☆ ☆ ☆ ☆ ☆ ☆

laws
☆ ☆ ☆ ☆ ☆ ☆ ☆

peace
☆ ☆ ☆ ☆ ☆ ☆ ☆

dream
☆ ☆ ☆ ☆ ☆ ☆ ☆

Dr. Martin Luther _____, Jr., had a _____ that all people could live, work, and play in _____. He gave speeches to help change _____ that were not fair. He believed that everyone should be treated the _____. We honor this great leader on his birthday, _____.

·········A Parade Of·······
Prominent Black Americans

Background For The Teacher
Booker T. Washington

In 1856 Booker T. Washington was born in a slave cabin on a Virginia plantation. When Booker was nine years old, slavery ended. His family moved to West Virginia where Booker's mother worked as a servant, and Booker, his brother, and their new stepfather worked in a salt mine. More than anything else, Booker wanted to learn to read—something no one in Booker's family could do. Booker's mother gave him some old schoolbooks, and Booker began to teach himself. When a teacher started a school nearby, Booker attended for a short time, but soon his stepfather needed him to work in the coal mines. In the mines is where Booker heard about a special school in Hampton, Virginia, that was especially for black students. When Booker learned that poor students could work at the school to pay for all or part of their education, he set his sights on attending school in Hampton.

When Booker was 16, he left home and entered Hampton Institute. He cleaned buildings and classrooms to pay for his tuition. During his time at Hampton, Booker learned many different jobs and subjects. After he graduated in June 1875, Booker became a teacher. Before long he was asked to be a principal at a new school for black students in Tuskegee, Alabama. When he arrived in Tuskegee, he learned that he was the school! There were no buildings, no teachers, and no students! But that didn't stop Booker. He began Tuskegee Institute in an old church. When Booker died in 1915, his school had grown to include more than 100 buildings! During his lifetime, Booker T. Washington became a famous teacher, the founder of an important school for black students, and the leading spokesman of African-Americans throughout the United States.

How To Use Page 33

1. Introduce students to Booker T. Washington (see the "Background For The Teacher: Booker T. Washington" and "Book Corner" on this page).
2. As a class discuss Washington's boyhood, adult life, and accomplishments; then have each student answer the questions about Booker T. Washington on the reproducible.
3. Ask each student to draw and color a picture of himself in the empty box, and to write his full name to the left of his picture.
4. Have each student complete the remainder of the page by following the provided directions.
5. If desired, set aside time for students to share their completed work with their classmates.

Background For The Teacher
Black History Month

Black History Month was started as a way of remembering the past, as well as the current, achievements of Black Americans. Dr. Carter G. Woodson, a black historian, is known as the Father of Black History. He suggested a Negro History Week in 1926. In the 1970s, his idea became Black History Week. Finally, in 1976, February was established as Black History Month.

Book Corner
Booker T. Washington

More Than Anything Else • Written by Marie Bradby & Illustrated by Chris K. Soentpiet • Orchard Books, 1995

First Biographies: *Booker T. Washington* • Written by Jan Gleiter and Kathleen Thompson & Illustrated by Rick Whipple • Steck-Vaughn Company, 1995

Booker T. Washington: Educator And Leader • Written by Jack L. Roberts; includes photographs • The Millbrook Press, Inc.; 1995

Name _____

A Longing To Learn

Booker T. Washington

Answer the questions.

1. As a boy, what did Booker most want to learn? _____

2. Why did Booker want to learn to read? _____

3. How did learning to read change Booker's life? _____

4. How did Booker help others? _____

Answer the questions.

1. What do you most want to learn? _____

2. Why is learning this one thing so important to you? _____

3. How will this knowledge change your life? _____

4. How do you plan to help others? _____

Bonus Box: On the back of this sheet, write two ways that you are like Booker T. Washington. Then write one thing that reading about Booker T. Washington has taught you.

A Parade Of Prominent Black Americans

Background For The Teacher
Maya Angelou

In January 1993, when Maya Angelou read her poem for Mr. Clinton's presidential inauguration, Americans across the land listened. Her rich, deep voice captivated her listeners. She was reading a poem that she had written for the soon-to-be president of the United States. And her poem carried an important message of hope to all Americans.

Maya Angelou was born in St. Louis, Missouri, on April 4, 1928. After her parents divorced, she moved to Stamps, Arkansas. She and her brother Bailey lived with their grandmother. Maya's given name is Marguerite Johnson. But her brother always called her "mya sister" and later just "Maya." Maya has used her special nickname all her life. She began using the name Angelou when she became a singer.

When Maya was growing up, African-Americans were often not treated fairly. Blacks were usually not offered jobs that paid high wages. Black and white children did not go to the same schools. The town of Stamps was divided into the "white" section and the "colored" section. Maya rarely went to the white section of town. She learned early in life about prejudice—like the time a white dentist refused to treat her painful toothache because of the color of her skin.

Maya enjoyed waiting on customers in her grandmother's store. But she liked to read even more. She read many books by famous authors. Her favorite author was William Shakespeare. She would escape to other worlds through books. Going to church was also an important part of Maya's early life. Maya loved to sing.

Maya overcame many difficulties. As a teenager, she lived with her mother in California. She was not allowed to apply for a job collecting fares on a streetcar because of her race. But Maya did not give up. Each day she returned, until one day she was hired. She became that company's first black employee in San Francisco. As a young adult, Maya often worked as a cook or a singer to support herself. But she never stopped reading and believing in herself.

A famous black author once told Maya to write about her life. And that is what she did. She has since become very well-known for her autobiographies. Maya has used her creative talents in other ways, too. She is an actress and a teacher who can speak six different languages! This poet, author, and educator continues to influence the world around her through the magic and power of her words.

How To Use Page 35

To introduce youngsters to Maya Angelou, read aloud the information in "Background For The Teacher" on this page. Answer your students' questions and invite their comments. Next distribute student copies of page 35. Guide students through the activity; then provide paper on which students can write and illustrate their poetry. If desired, mount the youngsters' completed works on colorful construction paper and display them on a bulletin board titled "It's A Glorious Day!"

Sample Poem

Good Morning!

Alarm buzzing
Cat
Dog
Everything's funny.

Grapes
Juice
Lunch making.

Outdoors
Racing
Silly waving.

Name _____

Each New Day

Maya Angelou is a famous writer.
She wrote a poem for President Clinton.
Maya's poem was about bringing
   people of all races together.
Maya wants people to feel joyful about
   each new day.

Write an alphabet poem called "Good Morning!"
On the lines, write words that make you think of a
   new day.
Try to think of one word for each alphabet letter.

a _____   n _____

b _____   o _____

c _____   p _____

d _____   q _____

e _____   r _____

f _____   s _____

g _____   t _____

h _____   u _____

i _____   v _____

j _____   w _____

k _____   x _____

l _____   y _____

m _____   z _____

Choose 12 or more words from your list.
On another sheet of paper, copy the words in ABC order to create a very special
   poem.
Illustrate your poem.

A Parade Of Prominent Black Americans

Background For The Teacher

Sidney Poitier

Sidney Poitier is an American motion-picture actor who rose from poverty to stardom, and became a symbol of the breakthrough of black performers in American-made films. Born in 1927, Poitier studied acting at the American Negro Theater in New York while working there as a handyman. Racial discrimination limited Poitier to minor roles for many years, but he never lost the pride he had in himself and his race. In 1963 Poitier was a number-one box-office attraction. Three of his films—*To Sir With Love*, *Guess Who's Coming To Dinner*, and *Lilies Of The Field*—grossed over $62 million. He won an Academy Award for his performance in *Lilies Of The Field*. Poitier was the first black man ever to be nominated for and win this prestigious acting award. Poitier has since acted, directed films, and written his autobiography.

How To Use Page 37

Provide a copy of page 37 for each child. Direct students to read the information about Sidney Poitier and answer the reading comprehension questions.

Answer Key For Page 37

1. He lived on Cat Island in the Caribbean.
2. He went to school in Nassau.
3. He went to acting school. He acted in plays and movies.
4. He dreamed of having a better life.
5. He said he would never be in a movie that would embarrass his race.
6. He was the first Black American man to win the Academy Award for best actor.
7. Answers will vary.
8. Answers will vary.

Name _____

A Man Of Pride

Sidney Poitier was born in 1927. He was the eighth child born in his family. His family was very poor. They lived on Cat Island in the Caribbean. Cat Island had no electricity. There were no indoor bathrooms. There were no cars. There were no schools.

When Sidney was 11, his family moved to Nassau. They were still poor. Sidney started school, but he did not like it. Sidney loved to go to movies. He always dreamed of having a better life.

When Sidney was 17, he moved to New York. He wanted to be an actor. He practiced hard. He went to a school for actors. He acted in plays. Then he acted in movies. He said he would never make a movie that would embarrass his race.

Sidney became a star. In 1963, he won an Academy Award for best actor. He was the first Black American man ever to win this award. He starred in many more movies. His dream of a better life came true. And he always kept the pride he had in himself and in his race.

Answer the questions below.

1. Where did Sidney Poitier spend the early years of his life?_____

_____

2. Where did he go to school?_____

_____

3. What did he do in New York?_____

_____

4. What did Sidney Poitier dream of? _____

_____

5. What kind of movie did he say he would never be in?_____

_____

6. What did he become the first Black American man to do?_____

_____

7. Would you like to be an actor or an actress? Explain your answer._____

_____

8. If you could act in a movie, what kind of movie would it be? Explain your answer._____

_____

A Parade Of Prominent Black Americans

Background For The Teacher
George Washington Carver

George Washington Carver, a black American scientist, is noted for his research in agriculture, especially his work with peanuts. During his years of work Carver found over 300 uses for the peanut. Carver also worked to improve the relations between blacks and whites.

Carver was born in Diamond, Missouri, as a slave. Orphaned young, his owners, Moses and Susan Carver, raised him and taught him to read and write. At age 11, George moved to Neosho, Missouri, to attend a school for black students.

Carver worked hard to support himself throughout his school years. He earned a bachelor's degree in agriculture in 1894 and a master's degree in 1896. Carver then moved to Alabama and joined the faculty of Tuskegee Institute, a school for blacks studying agriculture and industry. Carver first specialized in the studies of fungi, later directing his time to soil conservation and crop production. He wrote and distributed many pamphlets on applied agriculture. He also taught his practices through conferences, exhibits, demonstrations, and lectures.

In 1910, Carver turned his studies to the peanut. He became well known after he gave a lecture to a committee of Congress. He became very active working for the Commission on InterRacial Cooperation and the Young Men's Christian Association (YMCA).

Carver received many awards throughout his time for his numerous achievements and advancements in agriculture. The George Washington Carver National Monument was established in 1951 on the farmland where Carver was born.

Materials Needed To Make A Mr. Peanut Card:
— scissors
— light brown construction paper

How To Use Page 39
Duplicate the sheet on light brown construction paper. Demonstrate steps. Provide assistance if needed.

Directions For Students
1. Cut along the outer solid line.
2. Fold on the dotted lines so Mr. Peanut's face is showing.
3. Cut on the solid inner lines.
4. Write a peanut poem inside the card.

Variations
— Write a favorite peanut recipe inside the card and give it to a friend.

— Write a list of all the different things that peanuts can be used for on the inside of the card. Remember, George Washington Carver found over 300 uses!

— Enlarge the peanut card and use it as a center. Program it with math facts, reading comprehension, or language activities.

— For a bulletin board, draw a large peanut plant. Place the cards on the roots to show that peanuts grow underground. On the plant leaves, label the many different uses for peanuts. Uses include:

peanut butter	machinery oil	soap
face powder	shaving cream	shampoo
paint	dressings	margarine
vegetable oils	animal feed	plastics
cork substitutes	wallboard	abrasives

Name _____

"Mr. Peanut" Card

George Washington Carver discovered over 300 different uses for the peanut, from peanut butter to cattle food. Remember his achievements by making your own "Mr. Peanut" card.

A Parade Of
Prominent Black Americans

Background For The Teacher
Harriet Tubman

A former slave, Harriet Tubman helped more than 300 other slaves escape during the 1850s via the famous Underground Railroad. Harriet was born Araminta Ross, in Bucktown, Maryland, around 1820. But she was most often called by her mother's name, Harriet. Her father taught her about surviving in the woods, knowledge that later became vital when she led slaves to escape. Harriet began helping others early in life. At age 13 she tried to save another slave from being punished. Her owner threw a heavy weight at her, and she suffered a severe wound. For the rest of her life she suffered blackouts.

Harriet married John Tubman, a freed slave, in 1844. Several years later, in 1849, she escaped slavery and worked as a hotel maid in Philadelphia. Shortly thereafter she became a *conductor* on the Underground Railroad and led others to freedom. Rewards for her capture totaled as much as $40,000. She made at least 15 Underground Railroad trips and never lost a slave. She led her brothers and her parents to freedom.

During the Civil War Harriet worked as a nurse and spy. On one rescue mission she helped free more than 750 slaves from prison. Later in life she became involved in the fight for women's rights, and she opened a home for aged Black Americans. Harriet Tubman died in 1913.

How To Use Page 41

Provide a copy of page 41 for each child. Direct students to read the information about Harriet Tubman and answer the questions.

Answer Key For Page 41
1. Answers will vary.
2. Answers will vary.
3. She was a nurse and a spy.
4. She raised money for black schools. She started a home for black people who were old or in need.
5. Answers will vary.
6. Answers will vary.

Fighting For Freedom

Harriet Tubman was a brave woman. She was born a slave in Maryland. When she was older, she escaped to freedom. Harriet wanted to help free other slaves, too. But it was a crime to help a slave.

Harriet Tubman became a leader of the *Underground Railroad.* This was not a real railroad. It was not even underground. It was a secret way to help slaves reach the free states. Harriet helped free hundreds of slaves.

During the Civil War, she worked for the Union Army. She was a nurse and a spy. After the war she helped raise money for black schools. Harriet Tubman also started a home for black people who were old or in need.

Answer the questions.

1. Why was Harriet Tubman considered brave? _____
_____
_____

2. Why do you think Harriet Tubman risked her life to help other slaves? _____
_____
_____

3. What were her jobs for the Union Army? _____
_____
_____

4. What did Harriet Tubman do after the war? _____
_____
_____

5. What do you think it means to be a slave? _____
_____
_____

6. How would your life be different if you did not have freedom? _____
_____
_____

Black History Bingo

Materials Needed:

—scissors
—glue
—peanuts
— crayons
— Ziploc® bag

How To Use Pages 42–43 To Play Bingo

Duplicate and cut apart a copy of the patterns below to use as calling cards. Store cards in a Ziploc® bag when not in use. Provide students with construction paper copies of the open bingo card on page 43 and the game pieces below. Have students color and cut out their game pieces. Then, to create a bingo card, have the students glue their game pieces in random order on their grids.

Directions For Play

1. Provide each student with a supply of peanuts (in honor of George Washington Carver) to use as markers.
2. Have each student cover the free space on his card with a peanut.
3. Shuffle the calling cards and place in a stack facedown on a table.
4. Draw the cards one at a time, calling out the name featured on each one.
5. Have students place peanuts on the matching spaces of their bingo cards.
6. When a student has marked five spaces in a row (either vertically, horizontally, or diagonally), he calls, "Bingo!"
7. To culminate the activity, allow students to eat their game pieces!

Game Pieces

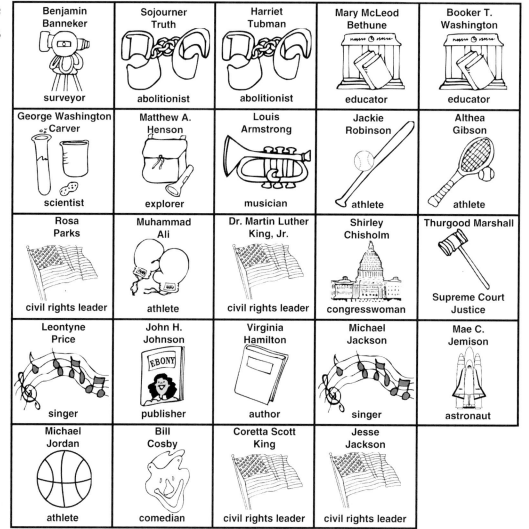

Benjamin Banneker — surveyor	Sojourner Truth — abolitionist	Harriet Tubman — abolitionist	Mary McLeod Bethune — educator	Booker T. Washington — educator
George Washington Carver — scientist	Matthew A. Henson — explorer	Louis Armstrong — musician	Jackie Robinson — athlete	Althea Gibson — athlete
Rosa Parks — civil rights leader	Muhammad Ali — athlete	Dr. Martin Luther King, Jr. — civil rights leader	Shirley Chisholm — congresswoman	Thurgood Marshall — Supreme Court Justice
Leontyne Price — singer	John H. Johnson — publisher	Virginia Hamilton — author	Michael Jackson — singer	Mae C. Jemison — astronaut
Michael Jordan — athlete	Bill Cosby — comedian	Coretta Scott King — civil rights leader	Jesse Jackson — civil rights leader	

Boning Up On Black History

Make a bingo card.
Cut and paste the pieces.

		free		

More About
Dr. Martin Luther King, Jr.

How To Use Page 45

1. Read aloud a picture book that tells about the boyhood, adult life, and dreams of Martin Luther King, Jr. (see "Book Corner"). Discuss the story.
2. Ask students what they can learn from Martin Luther King, Jr.'s experiences.
3. Create a class-generated list of Martin Luther King, Jr.'s positive traits. Discuss how these traits can have a positive influence on others.
4. Ask youngsters what makes a person a positive role model. Lead students to understand the numerous ways which Martin Luther King, Jr., is a positive role model.
5. Have each student complete page 45 by following the directions provided.

Book Corner
Martin Luther King, Jr.

Happy Birthday, Martin Luther King • Written by Jean Marzollo & Illustrated by J. Brian Pinkney • Published by Scholastic Inc., 1993

Martin Luther King • Written by Rosemary L. Bray & Illustrated by Malcah Zeldis • Greenwillow Books, 1995

My Dream Of Martin Luther King • Written & Illustrated by Faith Ringgold • Crown Publishers, Inc.; 1995

Extension Activity

Dr. King encouraged people to work for what was right in a peaceful way. Bring the spirit of Dr. King's teachings into your classroom with this inspirational display. Mount a dove cutout and the title "Joining Hands For Peace" near the center of a bulletin board. Have each student trace his hand on colorful construction paper and cut out the resulting shape. Then, on his cutout, each child writes his name and describes how he can help make the classroom a friendly place. Mount the students' completed projects around the dove cutout for a "hand-y" reminder of Dr. King's dream. If desired weave a yarn length adorned with construction-paper leaves among the cutouts as shown.

A Man With A Dream

Dr. Martin Luther King, Jr., dreamed of a peaceful world.
He worked hard to make his dream come true.

Follow the directions.
Write your ideas in the cloud shapes.

List Dr. King's positive traits.

Describe what you like best about Dr. King.

Tell one thing Dr. King has taught you.

Martin Luther King, Jr.
1929–1968

Compare yourself to Dr. King.

Explain why you think Dr. King is a good role model.

Bonus Box: On the back of this paper, draw and color a person who is a role model to you. Write who the role model is and describe how this person encourages you to be the best that you can be.

45

More About
Dr. Martin Luther King, Jr.

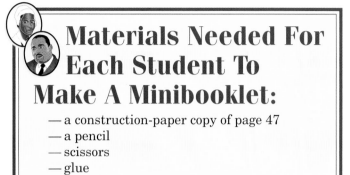

Materials Needed For Each Student To Make A Minibooklet:

— a construction-paper copy of page 47
— a pencil
— scissors
— glue

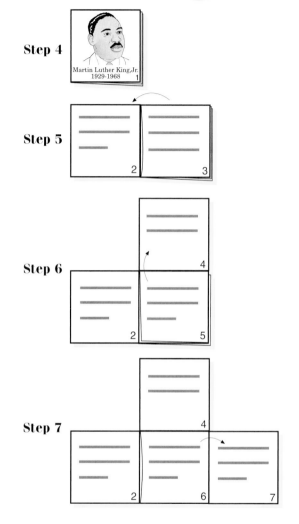

How To Use Page 47

1. Read aloud a picture book that tells about the boyhood, adult life, and dreams of Martin Luther King, Jr. (see "Book Corner" on page 44). Discuss the story.
2. Distribute the materials listed above.
3. Have each student decode the words in the Word Box by following the provided directions.
4. Under your students' guidance, identify each decoded word and allow students to correct their work as needed.
5. Instruct each child to use her decoded words to complete the sentences about Martin Luther King, Jr.
6. One at a time, enlist a different student to read each completed sentence aloud. Allow students to correct their work as needed.

Minibooklet Assembly

1. Cut out the large nine-box square along the bold lines.
2. Cut away boxes 1, 3, 5, and 6 by cutting along the dotted lines. Set the resulting single pages aside.
3. Position the larger cutout in front of you. Page 4 should be at the top. Fold the four outer boxes, or pages, inward along the thin lines in the following order: page 9, page 7, page 4, page 2.
4. Glue the page 1 cutout to the resulting minibooklet cover.
5. Open the cover and glue the page 3 cutout to the blank surface that is to the right of page 2.
6. Open page 3 to reveal page 4. Glue the page 5 cutout to the blank surface below page 4.
7. Open page 5 and glue the page 6 cutout to the blank surface.
8. Allow time for the glue to dry; then refold the minibooklet, flip it over, and write your name on the back. (Provide assistance as needed.)
9. To read the minibooklet, open the pages one at a time and read them in sequential order.

How To Use Page 48

Duplicate a copy of page 48 for each of your students. Have students read the quote by Martin Luther King, Jr., and discuss its meaning. Encourage students to share their ideas about the importance of living in harmony and celebrating our differences. Then, on the lines provided, have each child write his own "I have a dream…" quote. Have students cut along the bold lines. Next provide them with a variety of discarded magazines. Have students cut out pictures showing friendship and/or people of various ethnic backgrounds, glue their pictures into collages on the top portions of their cutouts, and trim the collages along the edges. If desired, have each child glue his cutout to a sheet of 9" x 12" colored construction paper and then trim the construction paper to form a one-inch border around the cutout. Display the completed projects on a bulletin board or in your hallway.

A Memorable Man

Decode the words in the Word Box.
Change each letter to the letter that follows it in the alphabet.
Write the decoded word on the line.

Word Box

anqm	_____	bnkkdfd	_____
rgns	_____	odnokd	_____
qhfgsr	_____	fhudm	_____
rstcdms	_____	rbgnnk	_____
lhmhrsdq	_____	cheedqdmbd	_____

**Martin Luther King, Jr.
1929–1968**
©The Education Center, Inc.

1

Martin Luther King, Jr., went

to _____.

4

He became a _____

and a civil _____

leader.

5

Martin Luther King, Jr., was

_____ on

January 15, 1929.

2

In 1964 Dr. King was

_____ the

Nobel Peace Prize.

8

Dr. King chose peaceful

ways to try to make a

_____.

7

Martin studied very hard in

_____. He was a

very good _____.

3

In 1968 Dr. King was

_____ and killed in

Memphis, Tennessee.

9

Dr. King had a dream that all

_____ would

be treated equally.

6

Keep On Dreaming

"I have a dream that my four little children will one day live in a nation where they will not be judged by the color of their skin but by the content of their character."

—*Martin Luther King, Jr.*

I have a dream _____

_____

_____

_____

_____
name